PRINTING FOR LIFE

NOT JUST BYE !

Make it good! Stories for Life

Book Author: **Stories for Life**
Title: **Not just bye!**
© 2015 Printing for Life

All images © 2015 Printing for Life
(created by FAID Studios for Printing for Life)

ISBN-13: 978-09940339-0-1

NOT JUST BYE !

Make it good! Stories for Life

**What does it mean
to say goodbye
to someone
who makes you feel happy?**

It means that
sometime before
there was probably a 'hello'
with a warm hug and a big smile.

Imagine it is almost Christmas and your favourite
uncles and aunties have just arrived from their long trip
(half-way across the world)
to celebrate with you in your very own home.

Christmas holidays are your favourite
time of the year for many reasons:

So many people to play with
and spend time with, so many presents
and exciting activities.

Much sooner than you would like

_____

the expected happens:

Christmas is over.
But thankfully something else happens every year
after Christmas.

A few days
after Christmas,
on the last day of
the year ....

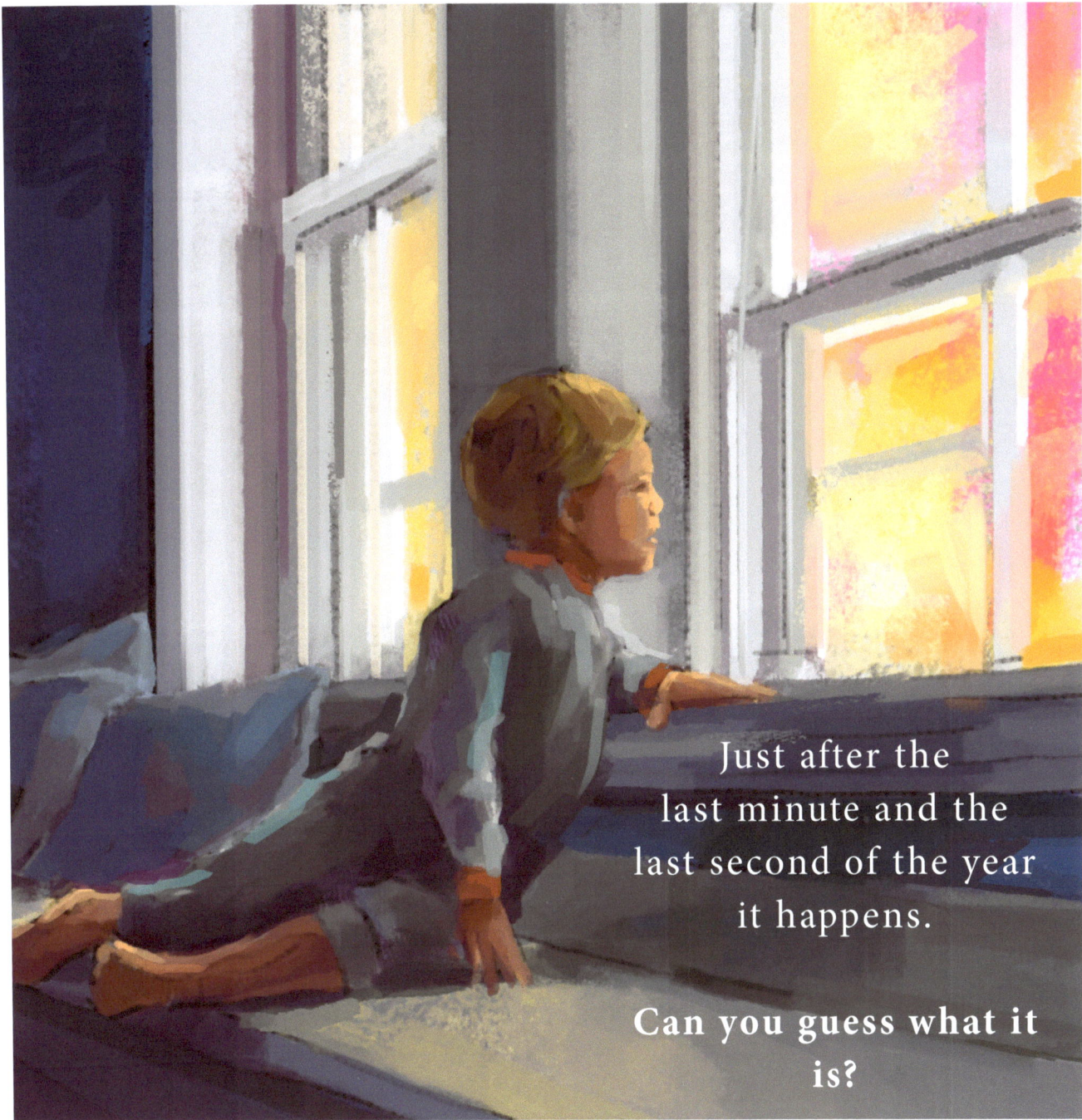

Just after the
last minute and the
last second of the year
it happens.

Can you guess what it
is?

Wooooooosh BANG!

A sky full of wonders:

fireworks bringing in the new year.

HAPPY NEW YEAR

Beautiful colours lighting up the night sky.

Fun shapes and forms.

Can you see, hear and smell it?

Soon after you hear the sounds of cheers and laughter,
well-wishes and toasting.
Not the type of toasting
you do with bread and a toaster.

This type of toasting involves raising
your glass and drinking together to wish someone well or
celebrate something
special. We'll come back to this
but first let's continue your story.

After toasting there is much cheering
and celebration!

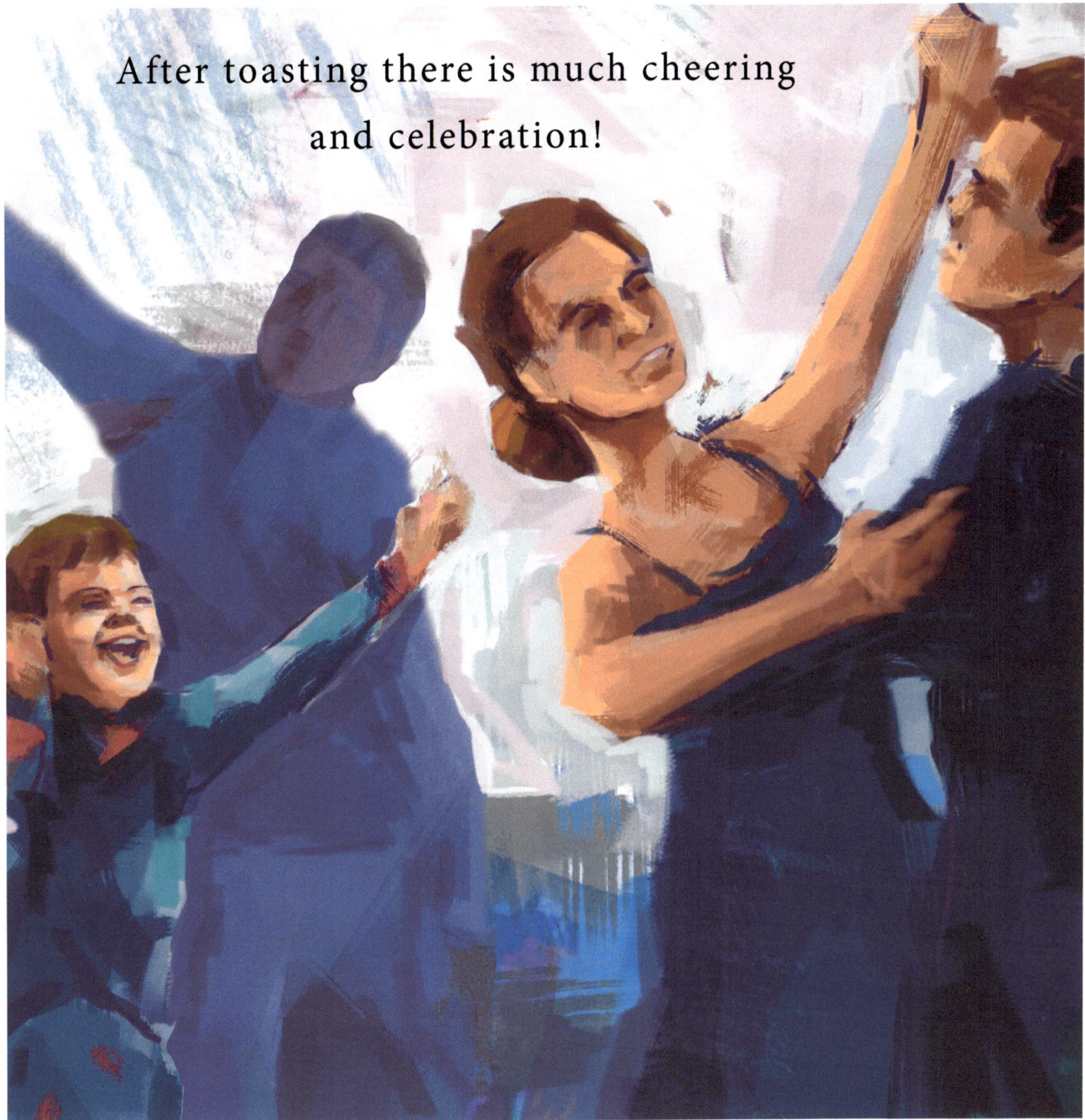

Soon it is time to switch off
the light and to everyone
say goodnight.

Saying goodnight is like
saying goodbye
to the day and hello to
the night.

You fall asleep. Can you hear yourself snore?

Wait a moment, something's happening.

Something is tickling your nose...

What's happening?

Where's that coming from?

The sun is beaming through the window

and tickling your nose....

Hatschu! Hatschu!

A loud sneeze!

Sorry two loud sneezes!

One after the other echoing through the room ...

All the way throughout the house...

Resulting in everybody waking up!

A new day! The first
day of
the New Year:

New Year's Day!

In our story this is the day to say goodbye to your favourite aunties and uncles because they have to travel back home half-way across the world.

That's a long way.

Saying bye isn't easy and doesn't feel nice,

when you have had such a good time.

But isn't it a little bit like saying goodnight?

How can you make saying bye good (a true `good´-bye)?

Does it become good through:
Head-butting your uncle?
Screaming at your aunty?
Kicking the door?
Running away?

Of course not! You're right.
But how do you make it so it's a real goodbye?
Any ideas? Do you remember the toast?

Well, here is an idea:
You can think about the three T's -
Think, Thank and Toast.

Think about the awesome time
You had together
Memories which last forever.

Thank 'em for being with you and
For making your wishes come true.

I suggest you make a **Toast**
(I don't mean offering crispy bread)
I'm talking about wishing them well
And making it a true farewell!

You're allowed to feel sad and blue
For a millisecond or two!
But then it's time
To end this rhyme
And focus on the coming time!

'Not just bye' is a beautifully illustrated and touching story that acknowledges and validates one of the challenges that children face: It is hard to say good-bye to loved ones and fun times. It is written from a child's perspective and is simple to understand; for example, it explains what a 'toast' is. Young children are just learning life coping skills and I believe that this book recognizes the difficulty of facing good-byes and also offers solutions to dealing with the same. This, in turn, will educate children in problem-solving in other areas of life.

Charis

PRINTING FOR LIFE

Printing for Life is a boutique publishing company which originated in Australia and developed further with editorial members based in Canada, the United States and Germany. Printing for Life was created to publish Stories for Life with children in mind, believing that a narrative can not only be entertaining and educational but also therapeutic at the same time. This concept is termed narrative medicine and has received increasing attention over the last decade. The stories published by Printing for Life are meant to connect the author and the reader, as well as the illustrator and editorial staff and to remind each one of their own life and purpose. That's why the series is called Stories for Life.

Saying goodbye can be challenging for children and adults alike.

How can you make saying 'bye' good?

In this captivating and beautifully illustrated story for children,

a young boy discovers an answer to this challenge.

Based on a real-life event.

ISBN 978-0-9940339-0-1

9 780994 033901

www.ingramcontent.com/pod-product-compliance
Lightning Source LLC
Chambersburg PA
CBHW042022090426

42811CB00016B/1707

In 2016, I started thinking about my diet with the intention of having a clean and healthy digestive system, and was coming to the conclusion that eating a whole foods plant based diet would be best for this intent.

Coincidentally, at the end of that year, I also had a conversation with someone which led me to look into how animal farming industries work ~ and this newly learned information made it an easy decision for me to stop using animals for food completely.

Going down this path of research made me think about my own relationship to animals, and question whether my decision to eat them was ever really my own choice, or just something that was normalized, passed down, promoted and socially conditioned for me to do. Deciding to take another path felt like gaining sovereignty over my own heart, mind and meals.

I know for a lot of people, changing their diets or even just keeping up with thier current one can feel like work. For me, because I already had a lot of experience working in different kitchen scenerios, and because I'm also someone who lives with a minimalist mindset and likes to simplify ~ changing my diet felt more like a creative project, than hard work.

If you are new to eating a plant based diet, new to cooking in general, or a seasoned vegan looking for some minimalist recipes, I made this book for you and I hope you enjoy many great meals from it.

Photography and Design by Jennifer Barbato

A note on the recipes: While I am not the original person to invent carrot ginger soup, the recipe in this book is my version, tailored to how I like it. All of the recipes in this book are like this. They come from all different origins, and from different times in my life ~ and I've adjusted them to be vegan, to fit my taste preferences, and to simplify the recipe and process where I could.

My Italian grandmother taught my mother how to make tomato sauce. My mother taught me. And I make it different than both of them. My Armenian step-father taught me how to make hummus, but I have my own way of making it now, that stems from, but is a little different than his.

The pancakes and zucchinni cake recipes came from when I worked as cook at a Bed & Breakfast, and I updated them to a vegan version. The tahini dressing came from a kitchen at a Vippassana Retreat. I didn't get the actual recipe, but made up my own based on trial and error when I got home.

The creme sauce was something I came up with trying to replicate a mac and cheese feel for my daughter, which she calls "special sauce". This might be the closest to an original recipe in this book. So again, while I may not have invented salad and a simple dressing, I wanted to share the particular way I do it, hoping you will enjoy it too.

KITCHEN

*You can have a fully functioning kitchen
with minimal equipment*

Basic Equipment

Tea pot

Soup pot

Pancake pan

Vegetable pan

Cutting board for fruit

Cutting board for vegetables

Glass baking dish

Wooden spoon

Spatula

Whisk

Large chopping knife

Serrated knife

Immersion blender

Cupcake tray

Colander

Grater

These are the foods I like to keep stocked
in my fridge, freezer and pantry

Fridge

Soy milk
Vegan butter
Tofu
Tempeh
Miso paste
Apple sauce
Tahini

Freezer

Raspberries
Mangos
Edamame

Pantry

Oatmeal
Unsweetened coconut flakes
Pumpkin seeds

Flour
Baking powder
Baking soda

Grains
Legumes
Pasta
Popcorn

Nutritional yeast
Dried herbs
Salt

Maple syrup
Apple cider vinegar
Tamari
Olive oil

There are so many grains, legumes
and milks to choose from

Grains

Brown rice

Wild rice

Black rice

Green rice

White rice

Quinoa

Amaranth

Polenta

Legumes

Black beans

White beans

Garbanzo beans

Pinto beans

Red beans

Mung bean

Split pea

Lentils

Milks

Soy milk

Rice milk

Almond milk

Coconut milk

Hazelnut milk

Hemp milk

Flax milk

Oat milk

These are my favorite fruits and vegetables

Fruits	Vegetables
Strawberries	Lettuce
Grapes	Spinach
Peaches	Asparagus
Plums	Mushroom
Watermelon	Leek
Banana	
	Cauliflower
Avocado	Broccoli
Lemon	Potato
Tomato	Yams
Cucumber	Carrot
Zucchini	Beet

BASICS

Cooking the basics is simple

PASTA

Bring a pot of water to boil. Make sure there is enough water so that you can fit the amount of pasta you are cooking with enough room for it to expand. The amount of time will depend on how much pasta you are cooking and what kind of pasta it is. For example, angle hair pasta will cook much faster than rigatoni.

RICE

Most rice is cooked at a 1:2 ratio. Meaning, one cup of rice to two cups of water. Add both the rice and the water in a pot. Add a pinch of salt. Bring the water to a boil, and simmer with the lid on until all the water is absorbed (usually 20 - 30 minutes). * Brown rice uses 1 cup of rice to 1 1/4 of water.

BEANS

Rinse beans and soak them for 5 - 8 hours. Drain and rinse. Put beans in a pot and add water. Make sure there is enough water for the beans to expand. Add salt and bring to a boil. Reduce to low heat and cook until soft. Cooking time depends on how much beans you are cooking.

LENTILS

Lentils do not need to be pre-soaked, only rinsed. Cook 1 cup of lentils to 1 1/2 cups of water. Add salt and bring to a boil. Cover and reduce heat. Cook until soft. Cooking time depends on how much lentils you are cooking.

ROASTED VEGETABLES

I roast all my vegetables the same way. I coat them in oil, sprinkle with salt, and bake them at 400 degrees until soft and browned.

My favorite vegetables to roast are potatoes, beets, yams, cauliflower & asparagus.

Dense vegetables such as yams will take more time than softer vegetables such as asparagus.

I like to cut potatoes, yams and beets into french fry size. I like to cut caulifower into very small pieces. Aparagus, I leave whole.

TOFU & TEMPEH

I use firm tofu and cut it into cubes. Tempeh, I cut into strips. Sauté in oil with a pinch of salt until browned.

MISO SOUP

Boil water in a tea pot. Put a tablespoon of miso paste in a soup bowl. Pour hot water over the miso paste and break it down with a fork until it's mixed in smoothly.

SIMPLE BROTH

Chop equal amounts of leeks, celery & carrots. Lightly cook the leeks and celery in a pan with sunflower oil and a pinch of salt. As the leek and celery are cooking, boil a pot of water. When the water boils, add the leek, celery and carrots to the pot and let simmer for 1 hour. Drain the liquid out and compost the veggies. I like to store my broth in mason jars.

RECIPES

Dry
1 cup flour
1 tsp baking powder
1/4 tsp baking soda
2 pinches of salt

Wet
1 cup unsweetened soy milk
splash of apple cider vinegar
1 tbs apple sauce

1 tsp vegan butter

PANCAKES

Combine and mix dry ingredients in one bowl. Combine and mix wet ingredients in another. Add the dry to the wet mix little by little, breaking up flour lumps. Do not over mix.

Melt vegan butter in pan. When the butter is hot, pour in your batter. When you see bubbles on your pancake, you can flip it and cook the other side. Serve with maple syrup or raspberry sauce.

1/4 cup frozen raspberries
1 tbs maple syrup
pinch of flour

RASPBERRY SAUCE

In a small pot or pan, heat up frozen raspberries with a splash of water. Wisk in maple syrup & a pinch of flour to thicken.

1 cup rolled oats
2 cups water

chopped almonds
toasted coconut flakes
maple syrup

OATMEAL BOWL

Combine rolled oats in pot with water. Bring to boil, cover, and cook on low heat until oats are soft.

I top with chopped almonds & toasted coconut flakes with just a touch of maple syrup.

1 package of firm tofu
1/2 of a leek
1 cup of spinach

1 tbs sunflower oil
pinch of salt

TOFU BOWL

Thinly slice the leek and sauté in sunflower oil & salt until soft.

Cube up the tofu and add it to the leeks to cook for another 7 - 10 minutes or until leeks and tofu are browned.

Add in 1 cup of spinach and stir in until it wilts down.

1/2 cup zucchini
1 tbs sunflower oil

Dry Bowl:
1 cup flour
1 tsp baking powder
1/4 tsp baking soda
2 pinches of salt

Wet Bowl:
1 cup unsweetened soy milk
splash of apple cider vinegar

1 tsp vegan butter

ZUCCHINI CAKES

Grate the zucchini and sauté in sunflower oil.

Combine and mix dry ingredients in one bowl. Combine and mix wet ingredients & sautéed zucchini in another.

Add the dry to the wet mix little by little, breaking up flour lumps. Do not over mix.

Melt vegan butter in pan. When the butter is hot, pour in your batter. When you see bubbles on your pancake, you can flip it and cook the other side. Serve with avocado.

ingredients

1 banana
3/4 cup mango
1/4 water
1 tbs maple syrup

MANGO SMOOTHIE

Put chopped banana & chopped mango in a pint size mason jar. Add water & maple syrup. Blend with an immersion blender or a regular blender.

Use more or less water depending on how thick you like your smoothie.

You can use fresh or frozen fruit. I usually use fresh banana and frozen mango.

ingredients

lettuce

arugula
sunflower sprouts
cucumber
avocado
cherry tomato
toasted pine nuts

MY BASIC SALAD

I always start with a base of lettuce. I love lettuce, and could simply eat a bowl of lettuce with dressing and be happy. But I also like to add a few more items such as:
arugula
sunflower sprouts
cucumber
avocado
cherry tomato
toasted pine nuts

When I'm extra hungry or cold, I love a big scoop of warm brown rice in my salad.

olive oil
lemon
nutritional yeast
salt

MY FAVORITE DRESSING

I don't pre mix this dressing. I just add one ingredient at a time into my salad and mix it all up. Adjust measurements to taste.

1 cup loosely packed fresh basil
1/4 cup tahini
1/4 cup water
3 tbs tamari

TAHINI BASIL DRESSING

Chop basil and combine ingredients a jar. Blend with an immersion blender or a regular blender. Add water to thin out if needed. Adjust measurements to taste.

1 small leek
1 tbs sunflower oil
pinch of salt

water
1/2 tsp salt

2 potatoes
3 carrots

1/2 cup spinach

SIMPLE VEGETABLE SOUP

In a pan, sauté leek in sunflower oil & salt.

In a medium sized pot, bring a little over a 1/2 pot of water to a boil with a 1/2 tsp of salt.

While waiting for the water to boil, chop potatoes & carrots. When the water is boiled, add the potatotes, carrots & sautéed leeks. Cook on low to medium heat until the potatoes and carrots are soft.

Turn off heat, and stir in a handful of spinach. Sometimes I blend it and sometimes I don't.

1 small **leek**
1 tsp **sunflower oil**
pinch of **salt**

water
1/2 tsp **salt**

2 **celery** stalks
4 - 5 **carrots**

1 large clove of **garlic**
2 tsp of **fresh ginger**

CARROT GINGER SOUP

Chop **leek** and sauté in a pan in **sunflower oil** & **salt**. Chop **celery** stalks and add to leeks when they are about half way cooked.

In a medium sized pot, bring a little over a 1/2 pot of **water** to a boil with a 1/2 tsp of salt. While waiting for the water to boil, chop **carrots** and add them to the pot when the water is boiled. Lower the heat to medium.

When the leek & celery are cooked down, add them to the pot. Then, thinly slice the **garlic** and sauté it in the pan being careful not to over cook it. You may need to add a little more oil. Before it browns, add it to the pot.

Then grate **fresh ginger** and add that to the pot too. When the carrots are soft, blend it with an immersion blender until smooth.

1 cup simple broth

1/2 leek
1 tbs sunflower oil
pinch of salt

1 1/2 cups mushroom

1 tbs flour

MUSHROOM GRAVY

Premake simple broth (recipe on page 20).

Thinly slice leek and sauté in sunflower oil & salt. Slice mushrooms. When the leeks are soft, add mushrooms with a little more oil and salt and cook until well done.

Add simple broth. Wisk in 1 tbs of flour (or more depending on how thick you want your gravy). Gently wisk while cooking for another 5-7 minutes.

You can blend the gravy if you want a smooth consistency. I like it both ways. Serve over roasted vegetables or rice.

1 avocado
1 tbs olive oil
1 tbs fresh lemon juice
2 pinches of salt

1/2 clove raw garlic

GUACAMOLE

Scoop out an avocado into a bowl. Add olive oil, lemon and salt. Mash up with a fork. Adjust measurements to taste. Serve with tortilla chips.

Sometimes I add 1/2 a clove of chopped raw garlic, and sometimes I don't.

1 cup cooked chickpeas
1/4 cup tahini
1/4 cup olive oil
1 tbs fresh lemon juice
2 pinches of salt
1/2 clove raw garlic

water to thin

HUMMUS

First you will need to soak & cook some chickpeas. Then, blend all ingredients.

Add water to get it to the right consistency. Serve with cucumbers, carrots and bread. I like it with toasted pita bread.

2 scallions
1 tbs sunflower oil
pinch of salt

1 clove garlic
3 tomatoes

1/4 cup fresh basil
pinch of salt
pinch of pepper

TOMATO SAUCE

Chop scallions and sauté in pan in sunflower oil & salt until they are soft.

Thinly slice garlic and add to the scallions when the scallions are cooked down. Be careful to not over cook the garlic.

Right before the garlic browns, add tomatoes. Add fresh basil, another pinch of salt & pepper.

Blend or leave as is. Serve over pasta.

ingredients

1 tbs of **vegan butter**
1/4 cup **unsweetened soy milk**
2 tbs of **nutritional yeast**
pinch of **salt**

CREME SAUCE

In a pot or pan, melt **vegan butter**, **soy milk**, **nutritional yeast** & **salt**. Serve over pasta.

ingredients

1 1/2 cups of **fresh basil**
2 tbs **olive oil**
1 tbs **fresh lemon juice**
1/4 tsp **salt**
1/4 cup **toasted pine nuts**

water to thin

PESTO SAUCE

Chop **basil** and put in your blender. Add **olive oil**, **lemon**, **salt**, **toasted pine nuts** and blend.

You can add a little water to smooth it out. Serve over pasta.

ingredients

1 tbs of **vegan butter**
1 **lemon**
pinch **salt**
2 pinches of **dried rosemary**

LEMON ROSEMARY SAUCE

Melt **vegan butter**. Add **lemon**, **salt** & **dried rosemary** . Mix and drizzle over grains, vegetables or tofu.

Dry
1 cup flour
1 tsp baking powder
1/4 tsp baking soda
1/4 tsp salt
1 tsp dried crushed rosemary.

Wet
1 cup unsweetened soy milk
splash of apple cider vinegar
2 tbs warm water
2 tbs olive oil.

1 pack of firm tofu
2 tbs sunflower oil
2 tbs fresh lemon jucie
2 tbs nutritional yeast
2 pinches of salt

ROSEMARY ROLLS

Combine and mix dry ingredients in one bowl. Combine and mix wet ingredients in another.

Add the dry to the wet mix little by little, breaking up flour lumps. Do not over mix.

Oil or butter cupcake tray and bake at 350 degrees for about 25 minutes.

BAKED TOFU

Cut tofu into cubes. Coat with oil, lemon, salt and nutritional yeast. Bake at 350 degrees for about 25 minutes.

1 cup **sushi rice**
2 cups **water**

1 avocado
1 cucumber

nori sheets
tamari
wasabi

SUSHI

In a pot, add **sushi rice** & **water**. Bring to a boil, cover, and then simmer until the water is absorbed.

When cooled, lay out a **nori sheet**. Make a strip of rice, a strip of sliced **avocado** and a strip of sliced **cucumber** on the nori sheet.

Roll it up tightly. You can use a special sushi roller or just use your hands. Slice it into pieces. Clean the knife with hot water in between rolls to prevent it from getting too sticky. Serve with **tamari** & **wasabi**.

Dry
1 cup flour
1/2 cup suger
I tsp baking powder
1/4 tsp baking soda
2 pinches of salt

Wet
1 cup unsweetened soy milk
splash of apple cider vinegar
2 tbs apple sauce
1 tbs melted vegan butter

1/4 cup vegan chocolate chips

APPLE CAKES

Combine and mix dry ingredients in one bowl. Combine and mix wet ingredients in another.

Add the dry to the wet mix little by little, breaking up flour lumps. Do not over mix.

Add chocolate chips.

Butter cupcake tray and bake at 350 degrees for about 25 minutes.

1 small zucchini
1 tbs of melted vegan butter

Dry
1 cup flour
1/2 cup sugar
1/2 cup cocoa powder
1 tsp baking powder
1/4 tsp baking soda
2 pinches of salt

Wet
1 cup unsweetened soy milk
splash of apple cider vinegar

CHOCOLATE ZUCCHINI CAKES

Grate zucchini and sauté in a pan with vegan butter.

Combine and mix dry ingredients in one bowl. Combine and mix wet ingredients in another.

Add the dry to the wet mix little by little, breaking up flour lumps. Do not over mix.

Add 1/3 cup of cooked zucchini.

Butter cupcake tray and bake at 350 degrees for about 25 minutes.

1 pack of fresh strawberries
1/4 cup vegan chocolate chips
splash of unsweetened soy milk

CHOCOLATE COVERED STRAWBERRIES

Melt chocolate chips in a pan or pot with a splash of unsweetened soy milk. Stir well being careful to not overcook the chocolate.

Dip strawberries in the melted chocolate. Eat warm, or put them in the fridge to harden.

1 cup dried coconut
pinch of salt
1 tbs agave

TOASTED COCONUT

Put dried coconut in a glass dish, sprinkle with salt, drizzle with agave and mix. Put it in the oven at 300 degrees. It will toast up fast so keep an eye on it so it doesn't burn.

1 avocado
2 tbs tamari

AVOCADO TAMARI BOWL

Slice an avocado in half, take out the pit, and pour tamari into the hole where the pit was. Eat with a spoon, using the avocado as the bowl.

2 tbs sunflower oil
1/4 cup popcorn
2 tbs vegan butter

salt
nutritional yeast
tamari
agave

POPCORN

Pour sunflower oil in a pot. Add popcorn. Cover and pop. In a separate pan, melt vegan butter and mix it in the popcorn.

I have a few different topping combinations I use:
• Salt & nutritional yeast
• Salt, nutritional yeast & tamari
• Salt & agave

May you find more peace, joy and freedom
through a simple vegan kitchen

Jennifer is a graphic designer with a background in fine art and photography. Born and raised in New York, she's worked for large companies, small businesses, and eventually for herself as a freelance artist and designer.

She has cooked for friends and family, private offices, retreat centers and Bed & Breakfasts' along the California Coast.

*This book is dedicated to
my mother, Patricia, and
my daughter, Evelyn.*

www.ingramcontent.com/pod-product-compliance
Lightning Source LLC
Chambersburg PA
CBHW042022090426
42811CB00016B/1708